THE

TWELVE-STEP

Workbook

of

Overeaters Anonymous

THE TWELVE-STEP *Workbook* of *Overeaters Anonymous*

OVEREATERS ANONYMOUS®

ISBN 0-9609898-5-4

Library of Congress Catalog Card No.: 93-83640

Overeaters Anonymous®, Inc.
6075 Zenith Court NE
Rio Rancho, New Mexico 87144-6424 USA
Mail Address: PO Box 44020
Rio Rancho, NM 87174-4020 USA
Tel: 1-505-891-2664
Fax: 1-505-891-4320
Web site: www.oa.org

Tenth printing 2004.

Printed in the United States of America.

PREAMBLE

OVEREATERS ANONYMOUS is a fellowship of individuals who, through shared experience, strength, and hope, are recovering from compulsive overeating. We welcome everyone who wants to stop eating compulsively. There are no dues or fees for members; we are self-supporting through our own contributions, neither soliciting nor accepting outside donations. OA is not affiliated with any public or private organization, political movement, ideology, or religious doctrine; we take no position on outside issues. Our primary purpose is to abstain from compulsive overeating and to carry this message of recovery to those who still suffer.

CONTENTS

INTRODUCTION

Welcome! You are about to begin a journey of self-discovery. Since the publication of *The Twelve Steps and Twelve Traditions of Overeaters Anonymous* book, OA members have expressed an interest in and a need for an accompanying workbook.

Although we all know the fourth step involves writing, many of us have found that writing on the other steps as well is more enlightening than working them "in your head." If writing intimidates you, remember that grammar and style are not important here—honesty is. You may be tempted to give a one- or two-word answer to the questions. However, it is suggested that you write down your feelings and thoughts as well.

The questions in this workbook were created directly from material in the first half of *The Twelve Steps and Twelve Traditions of Overeaters Anonymous* and are referenced accordingly. Some questions may not apply to you, or you may think of others to add.

There is no "perfect" way to use *The Twelve-Step Workbook of Overeaters Anonymous*. It is suggested for use with *The Twelve Steps and Twelve Traditions of Overeaters Anonymous*. You may wish to work with a sponsor, a workbook study group, or on your own. The sole purpose of the workbook is to guide your personal journey through the steps, and to explore and discover how compulsive overeating has affected your life, your relationships, and your well-being. It may also reveal how far you have come.

Completion of this workbook will take you not to the end of your journey, but to the threshold of a new dawning.

1

STEP ONE

We admitted we were powerless over food—that our lives had become unmanageable.

1. "In OA we are encouraged to take a good look at our compulsive eating, obesity, and the self-destructive things we have done to avoid obesity—the dieting, starving, over-exercising, or purging." Here is a first-step inventory of my compulsive eating history. (p. 3)*

My first real memory of compulsive overeating is at around age 6 or 7. I was with my grandparents on a Saturday because cartoons were on & I remember watching the Beatles cartoon. It was fall and I ate candy corn & they made caramel apples & I ate one & wanted another one & ate it, too. I think they were concerned, but let me eat it anyway. I also remember in nursery school eating two lunches. Even when the other kids went up for a nap, I'd still ask for another lunch. One of my big memories from nursery school is the "candy basket."

My mom remarried when I was 5 & I was already fat and I didn't like my new stepdad & I ate. Grandparents were a safe haven for me & always had plenty of goodies around.

When I got to college, I dieted & lost weight & started more of a binge/starve way to keep my weight down. I tried putting my fingers down my throat once, but I always hated throwing up, so luckily bulimia wasn't for me. In late 20's I also cut out food after food until I was a vegan for a few years, but still eating compulsively.

I lived abroad for many years & married an Israeli, Dani, & when we returned to Boston when I was 32, all the problems & angers at my parents/upbringing came crashing around me. Plus, I was not at all prepared for the "shark eat shark" world of music freelancing. I couldn't handle it & my weight, which I'd pretty carefully controlled for about 12-13 years at about 125 lbs, started climbing up & up to finally 240+ by age 47.

*Page numbers refer to *The Twelve Steps and Twelve Traditions of Overeaters Anonymous* (Rio Rancho, NM: Overeaters Anonymous, Inc. 1990), from which workbook questions were drawn.

a. What other solutions have I tried, and what were the results? Am I still looking for a solution outside OA? (p. 1)

1) Binge/starve – worked for about 12 years
2) Cutting out more & more food: first vegetarian, then vegan – worked but when we returned to Boston, I started to realize that these decisions were based on weight control, not personal or "for the animals" reasons & I ended up gorging on KFC one day & stopped being a vegan.
3) I thought if I could only make really interesting, gourmet meals, I'd be satisfied. – I did cook & bake well, & made lists of menu after menu. Lots of times I was just too tired or busy to prepare my fancy meal. Anyway, I would end up eating all the scones throughout the day. Didn't work. Never felt satisfied.

And even if I was satisfied, I wanted to eat 1 hour later again.

4) I also thought if I could have a dessert at each meal, I'd be satisfied or if I just had all this sweet stuff around I'd not care about it. Didn't work.

b. How have I used excess food to escape life's problems? (p. 2)

Oh, if I have any emotion, I want to eat. I could understand the bad emotions, but I didn't understand why I'd want to eat with happy emotions, too. I still don't quite understand, or maybe there's some other reason I don't get. When I was having so much trouble with freelancing, I'd would just eat & eat. I felt so sad & worthless & it took me all of the 1990s to climb out of allowing others to affect me so much, but I still lost the 240 lbs. I still eat compulsively today many times even though I'm in OA 6 months & have lost weight. I still worry and eat rather than pick up the phone or leave the house. I've continued to lose weight so I know I think I'm "getting away with it." You know, I'm 48. I just want to get it. I don't want to lose any more of my life to this disease.

c. Are there any particular foods or eating behaviors which give me trouble? (p. 2)

Used to be all sweets. This is my 3rd time back to OA, so I really have learned that the sweets are like alcohol for me & so far I've been very afraid & I haven't picked them up. But, I overeat on protein & I figure if I don't stop, it'll only be a matter of time until I say "What the hell? I'll have that cake." I know it'll lead to disaster & I don't want to go back there.

Bread, pasta, rice, I can take or leave. All the sweet baked things are my triggers. Eating when I'm emotional is a downfall, too. I also have trouble with the black & white of abstinence, as I've had to learn so much about the gray areas of life in my time here on Earth. I can't stand organized anything.

d. Have I returned to my former compulsive overeating behavior after years in recovery? (p. 2)

Not years, but few months, although I eat protein. I tell myself "It's like the South Beach diet, or Atkins, so it's OK." But I know for me, it's really NOT OK. My compulsivity makes it different. You can be compulsive with carrots for god's sake.

2. How has and does this malady affect my life not just physically, but emotionally and spiritually as well? (p. 3)

Not being able to wear a bathing suit without embarrassment. Not wanting to move physically with/for my kids - sports, walks, etc. I didn't grow up with active parents + swore I'd do things with my kids + I haven't kept that promise. Lost intimacy with husband. Always guilty about the food I ate, the sweets. Felt bad because I couldn't control myself. Felt/feel ugly, like a jerk, not worth living, not worth anything. Why am I here if I'm not leading the life I should lead? Why can't I just GET IT TOGETHER? Afraid if I can't, how will I be able to help my kids when they have challenges?

a. Have I excelled at my job or just gotten by? Explain. (p. 4)

As a bassoonist, yes I feel I'm pretty good. But I always feel underappreciated. Politics does play a big part, but I lost much of my BOS auditions to not thinking I was worth it or not good enough because I didn't get the positive feedback from others I always CRAVED. I had to learn that what they thought wasn't important. It was what I thought in the end. Long time + 125 lbs to learn it.

Now I don't know what to do. I'm tired of trying but the spark is still there. I need to simply go forward. Still in progress.

b. What has it been like living with me at home? (p. 4)

Dragon lady, Anger Queen. I'm now realizing that I must change my anger. I used to feel I "had to get it out," but now I read an online "rageaholics" website tailored around the 12 Steps and it says that we must completely abstain from anger. It makes sense. I want to think of ACTION instead of ANGER.

c. Has chronic unhappiness over my eating problems affected my friendships or marriage? How? (p. 4)

I don't know about friendships, but it has affected my marriage—lack of intimacy. We had a wonderful event this past summer, we had sex for the first time in 8 years, but it hasn't happened since. But before, I just felt too unattractive + unlovable I guess. Also, stress is a factor.

d. Am I in touch with my feelings, or have I buried my anger and fear in false cheerfulness? Explain. (p. 4)

I feel I'm in touch with my feelings. When I want to eat, I need to stop + immediately ask myself what's going in me + write it down. I am fearful about $ a lot. I dream of lots of money to be able to live with freedom + also to help others + I don't even handle my affairs now. Then I feel like a big fraud + I feel angry at God for giving me big wonderful dreams + no way to accomplish them.

3. How have I believed that my life would be manageable if only others around me would do as I wanted? Explain. (p. 4)

~~Well~~, Well, then I'd have power, right? My way is the right way. I wouldn't be sassed by my kids or questioned by my husband. And of course I'd be recognized finally for my great achievements and given more + more glory until I could take over for a retiring God. It's very ironic because I know that power corrupts most people. I know deeply that I'd be no different, yet I would still think I could handle it.

4. When and how has my life been unmanageable? (p. 5)

There have been times when ~~x~~ I couldn't stop eating the sweets - usually when there are just too many balls to juggle. At least I am not eating the sweets now nor the flour products. I feel my life is unmanageable when I'm idle. If I'm busy & my mind off of food, I can get a lot done & be abstinent!

5. Have I tried to control myself and wound up demoralized? Even when I succeed, has it been enough to make me happy? Explain. (p. 5)

Yes, sure, many times. I learned that because of my sugar addiction, my brain chemistry is set up wrong & no matter how much I am determined not to eat, I chemically am forced to, ~~x~~ totally against my will. Sometimes I wonder if it's also, with me, just a general food thing because I'm hungry again after one hour all the time, even with all protein & veg. I really do not eat sweets or bread. So why am I still having a "crash" feeling after a meal?

When I was thin, I was still way too insecure. I remember Delta Burke writing that when she was thin, she was a goddess & no one told her, so she didn't believe it. It was only after she gained weight & saw old photos of herself that she realized it. I agree. I had it all beauty wise & I didn't know it & was too insecure & naive to realize it.

I knew I was pretty, but didn't realize how insecure everyone else was. I thought it was my fault. I didn't have any foundation from my mom to handle this gift & I lost it.

6. Do I believe only an honest admission to myself of the reality of my condition can save me from my destructive eating? Why? (p. 6)

7. Do I acknowledge that my current methods of managing have not been successful, and I need to find a new approach to life? Explain. (p. 6)

8. Am I ready to change and to learn? Why? (p. 6)

9. Have I made an honest appraisal of my experience and am I convinced that I can't handle life through self-will alone? Explain. (p. 6)

2

STEP TWO

Came to believe that a Power greater than ourselves could restore us to sanity.

1. As I look with complete honesty at my life, how have I acted in an extremely irrational and self-destructive manner where eating is concerned? (p. 9)

2. In what ways have I been obsessed with diets and/or weight-loss schemes? (p. 10)

3. When those methods worked, how have I inevitably lost control and overeaten again, putting back on the weight I worked so hard to lose? Explain. (p. 10)

4. In what ways have I continued to try to find comfort in excess food, long after it began to cause me misery? (p. 11)

5. How have I not acted sanely when:

a. I yelled in response to my children's needs for attention? (p. 12)

b. I was jealously possessive of my mate? (p. 12)

5. How have I not acted sanely when:

c. I was more comfortable with food than with people? (p. 12)

d. I limited my social life? (p. 12)

5. How have I not acted sanely when:

   e. I drew the drapes, disconnected the telephone, and hid in the house? (p. 12)

6. In what ways have I overreacted to slight provocations while ignoring the real issues of my life? (p. 12)

7. Have I come to believe that I need to change? Why? (p. 12)

8. Since my willpower can't change my unsuccessful way of living, am I willing to look for a power greater than myself to restore me to sanity? (p. 12)

9. How do I define that Higher Power? (p. 13)

10. If I do not believe in a Higher Power, can I "act as if" I am getting help with my life? How? (p. 14)

11. What would I like such a power to be and to do in my life? (p. 14)

12. Do I believe in God but not really believe God can or will deal with my compulsive eating? (p. 15)

13. Have I asked God to remove my fat yet allow me to go on eating whatever I want? (p. 15)

14. How do I feel about replacing my old ideas about God with a faith that works? (p. 16)

15. What actions am I willing to take that others have told me worked for them? (p. 16)

3

STEP THREE

Made a decision to turn our will and our lives over to the care of God as we understood Him.

1. In what ways am I willing to adopt a whole new attitude about weight control, body image, and eating? (p. 20)

2. What has my attitude been about food and eating? (p. 20)

3. Am I ready to give up self-will regarding food? Explain. (p. 21)

4. How do I feel about completely turning my life over to a Higher Power for guidance? (p. 21)

5. Do I have eating guidelines? Will I ask God for the willingness and the ability to live within them each day? Explain. (p. 23)

6. If occasionally the obsession returns, how do I get through these times without overeating? (p. 23)

7. How do I reach the decision to turn my will and life over to a Higher Power? (p. 24)

8. Am I willing to earnestly seek God's will for me and willing to act accordingly? Explain. (p. 24)

9. What can I do when I feel unstable? (p. 25)

10. Why do I need to follow this new path? (p. 25)

11. What do I do when I face indecision? (p. 25)

12. What will it take for me to really work step three? (p. 26)

4

STEP FOUR

Made a searching and fearless moral inventory of ourselves.

1. Is something keeping me from beginning my "fearless" and "searching" inventory? What? (p. 30)

2. What action, no matter how small, am I willing to take to overcome my procrastination? (p. 31)

3. Am I willing to do a written inventory? (pp. 31-32)

4. What are some of the ways in which I can do my inventory? What approach will I take? (pp. 32-33)

5. Why is it important for me to take a balanced view of myself? (pp. 33-34)

6. Here is my fourth-step inventory guided by questions on pages 34 through 43 in *The Twelve Steps and Twelve Traditions of Overeaters Anonymous* and by reference to pages 64 and 65 in the Big Book, *Alcoholics Anonymous.* (pp. 34-43)

6. Here is my fourth-step inventory (continued). (pp. 34-43)

7. Now that I've written and reviewed my inventory, am I willing to ask God to help me add anything I may have left out? (p. 43)

5

STEP FIVE

Admitted to God, to ourselves, and to another human being the exact nature of our wrongs.

1. Now that I have finished my fourth-step inventory, how do I feel about sharing the details of my past with another human being? (p. 46)

2. Am I willing to be completely honest about the mistakes I have made? Explain. (p. 46)

3. How does my Higher Power help me leave rationalization behind and not blame others? (p. 46)

4. Have I gone back over my fourth-step inventory and acknowledged each truth about my past behavior, no matter how painful or embarrassing? (p. 46)

5. With whom will I share my inventory? (p. 48)
What are my reasons for this choice?

6. Am I willing to discuss the exact nature of my wrongs? (p. 49)

7. Why did I do some of the things I did? (p. 49)

8. What feelings led to my actions? What did I feel afterward? (p. 49)

9. What did these actions cost me? (p. 49)

10. In sharing my inventory with another, what did I learn about:

a. Fear? (p. 49)

10. In sharing my inventory with another, what did I learn about:

b. Trust? (p. 50)

c. Honesty? (p. 51)

10. In sharing my inventory with another, what did I learn about:

d. Acceptance? (p. 51)

6

STEP SIX

Were entirely ready to have God remove all these defects of character.

1. What is the difference between *saying* I'm entirely ready and *being* entirely ready? (p. 53)

2. Why is it so hard to be entirely ready to part with my defects? (p. 53)

3. Am I fearful? Do I feel I would be less interesting as a human being without some of my defects? Explain. (p. 54)

4. What are the choice defects that I would rather keep? (p. 55)

5. What does being "entirely ready" mean to me? (p. 55)

6. What do each of my defects do *for* me? (p. 56)

7. What do each of my defects do *to* me? (p. 56)

8. How has each of these old tools for coping with my life outlived its usefulness? (p. 57)

9. What harm is it doing me to cling to each of these ways of thinking and acting? (p. 57)

10. What do I believe is the essence of step six? (p. 57)

11. What is my attitude regarding change? (p. 58)

7

STEP SEVEN

Humbly asked Him to remove our shortcomings.

1. What is my concept of humility? (p. 59)

2. What is my self-image? (p. 59)

3. How does my self-image keep me from finding true humility? (p. 59)

4. What have I learned in OA about humility? (p. 60)

5. Why do I want God to remove my shortcomings? (p. 60)

6. Why is it important for me to accept each of my defects? (p. 61)

7. How can I let go of old attitudes which block humility, such as low self-esteem, status-seeking, and self-righteousness? (p. 62)

8. How do I complete step seven? (p. 62)

9. What is my list of defects? (p. 62)

10. How will I ask God to take my shortcomings from me? (p. 63)

11. Have I discovered other defects that I didn't see during the housecleaning I undertook in steps four through six? What are they? (p. 63)

12. How have I been shown what actions to take as a defect is removed? (p. 63)

13. What do I do when I make a mistake? (p. 64)

14. To what length am I willing to go in order to be rid of my shortcomings? (p. 64)

15. How do I cultivate the willingness to have any newly discovered fears, resentments, and other shortcomings removed? (p. 65)

16. Which character traits that have hurt me have become great assets when applied to the right things at the right times? (p. 65)

17. How has repeated practice of step seven affected my relationship with my Higher Power? (p. 65)

8

STEP EIGHT

Made a list of all persons we had harmed and became willing to make amends to them all.

1. In looking at my relationships, what patterns have I discovered that have done harm to me and others? (p. 67)

2. How do I identify what actually *is* harm to another person? (p. 68)

3. Whose names would I list from my fourth-step inventory as the people I have harmed? How have I harmed them? (p. 68)

4. Are there names on my list which may not belong there? Which ones? (p. 69)

5. Have I harmed myself? How? (p. 69)

6. What is my purpose in doing step eight? (p. 69)

7. How do I become willing to make amends to each person on my list? (p. 70)

8. What good suggestions have I received from my sponsor and other OA members to help me become willing? (p. 70)

9. What people on my list do I need to forgive for harms they have done me? (p. 71)

10. Why am I angry at each of these people? (p. 71)

11. Am I willing to give away what I have written to another person? (p. 72)

12. Am I willing to pray daily for those people who have wronged me so that I can be freed of my resentments and unforgiveness? (p. 72)

13. Am I *willing* to make amends even if I don't *want* to? (p. 73)

9

STEP NINE

Made direct amends to such people wherever possible, except when to do so would injure them or others.

1. Which amends have I put off making? (p. 75)

2. How has this immobilized me and threatened my recovery? (p. 75)

3. What are the dangers of doing more harm than good as I face people directly and talk with them about hurtful situations of the past? (pp. 75-76)

4. Have I talked with my sponsor or other person who understands the twelve-step way of life regarding my list of amends? (p. 76)

5. What is the purpose of step nine? (p. 76)

6. How is making amends more than just saying "I'm sorry"? (p. 76)

7. What expectations do I have of how the other people will receive me? (p. 76)

8. How will I give the victim of my wrong actions an honest and straightforward acknowledgment of my mistakes? (p. 77)

9. What sort of changes or restitution am I willing to undertake to set right my wrongs? (p. 78)

10. What are "living amends"? (p. 78)

11. To whom do I owe "living amends"? (p. 78)

12. How can I make it up to myself and my loved ones for the hurts of the past? (pp. 78-79)

13. To whom will I make direct amends? (p. 79)

14. How shall I make amends to those people I cannot find? Who are they? (p. 79)

15. How shall I make amends to those people who have died? Who are they? (p. 79)

16. What amends can I not make directly without harming somebody? (p. 80)

17. How can I make these amends anonymously to avoid hurting innocent people? (p. 80)

18. Are there any amends I want to make anonymously simply to avoid embarrassment to myself? Have I rationalized that making amends would injure me financially or damage my self-esteem? (p. 80)

19. How have I dealt with each person? (p. 81)

10

STEP TEN

Continued to take personal inventory and when we were wrong, promptly admitted it.

1. What actions do I take daily so that I may continue to experience recovery? (pp. 83-84)

2. How do I continue to work my program even during those times I feel it isn't working or I'm not recovering quickly enough? (p. 84)

3. What is the purpose of step ten? (p. 84)

4. What are the stumbling blocks that can keep me from growing today? (p. 84)

5. When do I need a spot-check inventory? (p. 85)

6. How do I do a tenth-step inventory? (p. 86)

7. What were the major events of the day? (p. 86)

8. What negative and positive feelings did I have? (p. 86)

9. How did I deal with those feelings? (p. 86)

10. What fears did I experience today, and how did I react to them? (p. 86)

11. When was I accepting and forgiving, letting go of former resentments? (p. 87)

12. When was I selfless? (p. 87)

13. What other positive character traits did I exhibit? (p. 87)

14. What were my true motives and emotions? (p. 87)

15. When was I wrong and promptly admitted it? (p. 87)

16. What actions can I take regarding the character defects found? (p. 87)

17. How willing am I to do a written daily inventory and occasionally share it with another OA member? (p. 87)

18. Do I need to do an extensive tenth-step inventory on a problem I was not aware of when I did my fourth step? (p. 88)

19. As I have grown in self-awareness, what areas of my past may I need to re-inventory? (p. 88)

20. On what particular character defect, behavior pattern, or area of life might I need to do an extensive tenth-step inventory? (p. 88)

21. In an effort to let go of a defect, how do I imagine I might behave if I did not have a particular defect? (p. 89)

22. Has the tenth-step inventory uncovered aspects of my past with which I need professional help? What are they? (p. 89)

23. What is my attitude regarding honesty about my problems and surrender to a power greater than myself? (p. 90)

24. In what ways am I grateful for this program? (p. 90)

11

STEP ELEVEN

Sought through prayer and meditation to improve our conscious contact with God as we understood Him, *praying only for knowledge of His will for us and the power to carry that out.*

1. How does step eleven challenge me? (p. 91)

2. What is my belief about recovery through a spiritual relationship with a power greater than myself alone? (p. 91)

3. In what ways do I actively seek to improve my relationship with my Higher Power? (p. 92)

4. How important is it for me to have a regular daily quiet time for prayer and meditation? (p. 92)

5. What do I say when I talk to God? (p. 93)

6. Am I afraid to express my honest feelings to God? When and why? (p. 94)

7. For what knowledge do I need to ask God? (p. 94)

8. When have I felt angry with God? (p. 95)

9. In what tangible ways can I communicate with God? (p. 95)

10. What is meditation? (p. 96)

11. What does meditation offer me? (p. 96)

12. How do I know which thoughts are God's directions and which are my own rationalizations? (p. 97)

13. How does time spent in prayer and meditation affect me? (p. 97)

14. What do I do when I feel I have received insight from my Higher Power? (p. 97)

15. What do I do when I need to make an important decision? (p. 97)

16. How do I respond when I make an error in acting on what I think is God's will for me? (p. 98)

17. In what ways does God speak to me? (p. 98)

18. What do I need to do to stay aligned with this higher spiritual power? (p. 98)

12

STEP TWELVE

Having had a spiritual awakening as the result of these steps, we tried to carry this message to compulsive overeaters and to practice these principles in all our affairs.

1. What has been my spiritual awakening experience? (p. 99)

2. What is the message of hope I have to carry to other compulsive overeaters? (p. 99)

3. How and why am I tempted to think that I have arrived at the end of my journey? (p. 100)

4. How am I to remain spiritually awake and fully alive? (p. 100)

5. In what ways have I tried to follow my program in isolation? (p. 101)

6. How has this affected my emotional balance and abstinence? (p. 101)

7. What have I experienced when sharing this program with other compulsive overeaters? (p. 101)

8. What part has service in OA played in my recovery? (p. 101)

9. How do I share my OA experience with other compulsive overeaters? (p. 102)

10. What expectations do I have regarding the outcome of this service to others? (p. 103)

11. How can I continue to practice my new way of acting upon life "in all my affairs"? (p. 103)

12. How do I confirm that I have turned my back on the old ways forever? (p. 103)

13. What did I learn about the following principles, inherent in each step, that I can practice in all my affairs:

a. Honesty in step one? (p. 103)

b. Hope in step two? (p. 104)

13. What did I learn about the following principles, inherent in each step, that I can practice in all my affairs:

c. Faith in step three? (p. 104)

d. Courage and integrity in steps four and five? (p. 104)

13. What did I learn about the following principles, inherent in each step, that I can practice in all my affairs:

e. Willingness in step six? (p. 104)

f. Humility in step seven? (p. 105)

13. What did I learn about the following principles, inherent in each step, that I can practice in all my affairs:

g. Self-discipline and love for others in steps eight and nine? (p. 105)

h. Perseverance in step ten? (p. 105)

13. What did I learn about the following principles, inherent in each step, that I can practice in all my affairs:

i. Spiritual awareness in step eleven? (p. 105)

j. Service in step twelve? (p. 106)

14. What footprints am I making for others to follow? (p. 106)

15. What is the message I am living? (p. 106)

THE TWELVE STEPS

1. We admitted we were powerless over food—that our lives had become unmanageable.

2. Came to believe that a Power greater than ourselves could restore us to sanity.

3. Made a decision to turn our will and our lives over to the care of God *as we understood Him.*

4. Made a searching and fearless moral inventory of ourselves.

5. Admitted to God, to ourselves, and to another human being the exact nature of our wrongs.

6. Were entirely ready to have God remove all these defects of character.

7. Humbly asked Him to remove our shortcomings.

8. Made a list of all persons we had harmed and became willing to make amends to them all.

9. Made direct amends to such people wherever possible, except when to do so would injure them or others.

10. Continued to take personal inventory and when we were wrong, promptly admitted it.

11. Sought through prayer and meditation to improve our conscious contact with God *as we understood Him,* praying only for knowledge of His will for us and the power to carry that out.

12. Having had a spiritual awakening as the result of these steps, we tried to carry this message to compulsive overeaters and to practice these principles in all our affairs.

THE TWELVE TRADITIONS

1. Our common welfare should come first; personal recovery depends upon OA unity.

2. For our group purpose there is but one ultimate authority—a loving God as He may express Himself in our group conscience. Our leaders are but trusted servants; they do not govern.

3. The only requirement for OA membership is a desire to stop eating compulsively.

4. Each group should be autonomous except in matters affecting other groups or OA as a whole.

5. Each group has but one primary purpose—to carry its message to the compulsive overeater who still suffers.

6. An OA group ought never endorse, finance, or lend the OA name to any related facility or outside enterprise, lest problems of money, property, and prestige divert us from our primary purpose.

7. Every OA group ought to be fully self-supporting, declining outside contributions.

8. Overeaters Anonymous should remain forever nonprofessional, but our service centers may employ special workers.

9. OA, as such, ought never be organized; but we may create service boards or committees directly responsible to those they serve.

10. Overeaters Anonymous has no opinion on outside issues; hence the OA name ought never be drawn into public controversy.

11. Our public relations policy is based on attraction rather than promotion; we need always maintain personal anonymity at the level of press, radio, films, television, and other public media of communication.

12. Anonymity is the spiritual foundation of all these traditions, ever reminding us to place principles before personalities.

For more information on Overeaters Anonymous
or for a copy of OA's literature catalog, write to
the World Service Office, PO Box 44020,
Rio Rancho, NM 87174-4020 USA.